Poetry Of The Damned

Or the Secret Lives of Vampires

Carey Millsap-Spears

/ BookLeaf
Publishing

India | USA | UK

Made with ❤ on the BookLeaf Publishing Platform
www.bookleafpub.in
www.bookleafpub.com

Dedication

For the Varney Club and PCA Vampires

Preface

This collection comes from various popular culture versions of vampires, from the recesses of my mind, and from some of the empty spaces in my heart.

Acknowledgements

Thanks for reading early drafts Sandy, Eric, Christy, and Matt.

This book was made possible because of the members of Hobart Creative Writers: Joe, Rachel, Bunny, Cristin, Gordon, and Heather. Many thanks for the inspiration and friendship and encouragement. Our group meets monthly at our local bookstore, Green Door Books, and it is a wonderful place. Thanks Jess!

Finally, I would like to thank all the vampires I have loved!

"It's Such a Little Thing to Weep"

After a line from Emily Dickinson

A little weeping
keeps me focused, grounded.
on the story, my story.

I weep single tears.
Each one holds back
the dam temporarily.

Sometimes, tears flow
all night.

Sometimes,
I'm all right.

A Down-Low Vampire

A truck-stop Vampire
wears plaid
instead of black.
Long ago, he traded his velvet cravat

for soft denim.
He sits perpetually alone
and keeps a gentle
lookout for his next ride,

his next bite.
His doe eyes, downcast,
lure the uneasy ones—
the cloistered ones

the ones who never talk
or cry out.
This Vampire knows
which trucker

to touch, to track,
to ask for a lift.
His hunting instincts sharp,
hardened—

calculated.

He runs his tongue over

the tip

when the right one comes along.

I, the Damned

In the future, maybe Vampires are gone–
They might be cured.

They might have been exposed,
found out. Ejected from shared spaces–
forced to remain immobile for eternity.
The threat of them eradicated,
erased.

They might be naked and alone,
floating through space with icicles
in their eyelashes.

A potential world without them seems
less colorful, less dramatic–
more utilitarian, more gray,
yet, today, I remain.

When Vampires Want to Die Young

Each day of my pitiful two-thousand-year-old
existence replays on a secret reel in my mind.

An eternal Monday grinds along.

To be forever
gives so many newly born creatures feelings of joy.

For me, I know the real toil is living without.

Living without connections or tethers
sometimes provides freedom, but

every face seems to look the same,
except for the one I miss the most: yours.

Midwest Vampires Bite, Differently

Outside a coffee shop near midnight,
one passes me, I know it.

"Ope," he says while sliding
across the threshold into the almost
empty cafe.

Offended, and a little tipsy, I place a hand
on the door, with a lippy whine, I cry:

"Why would he pass this fine
morsel by?"

I enter the space, scan the scene.
The lonely barista,
with two long teeth
replies, silently.

"Midwestern vampires bite,
differently."

What does that mean,
I wondered internally.

"We only want our own,"
the barista replied vocally.

Seemingly rejected from a chance
at immortality, I stare into the cloudy
windows and wonder:

"How did he know I wasn't from here?"

The barista sighs and rolls an eye,
"Is this for here or to go?"

The Golden Rule

Craving a neighbor
sounds too dirty
seems mighty dangerous—

So consider doing
unto others by
loving a neighbor.

It's much more
virtuous—
but overly monotonous.

Sharing a cup of sugar
wins smiles from
the block, yet

devouring a neighbor
only offers a new recipe
for the next party or church potluck.

The good book says
resist temptations
and make it to heaven,

but possessing my neighbor
gives me a second home
and a bigger television.

Dinner Time

It's a dreamy twilight.
It's time for us to wake.

The table is laid, ready for
the main event. I hesitate–

yet my everlasting hunger
pushes me to forsake
what's left of my humanity.

Murmurs, whimpers, and soothing
words rise,
lofting in from our kitchen.
They feel like aromas from a bygone time.

The ritual nears.

The chains clank. The sacrifice emerges,
and, as always, the willing one reconsiders
right before the first bite.

With an ever-brooding heart
and a deeply pallid eye

I sit, watch, and wait before
I, too, partake.

My family eats a now-silent meal
interrupted occasionally with a few crunches and slurps.
The fading purple sky
our only conscious witness.

I never tell the
truth about us.
I never reveal
how we came to be.
I never tell how we joined
our lives, eternally.
I never tell how ones so unnatural
became a family.

Well, tell me, could you?

We Never Go Out of Style

Spring cleaning, for vampires, takes on
new meaning every year.

I attempt to remember my many days
while sorting stockpiles of wedding
bands, varsity jackets, and books.

Deciding what to keep
what to toss,

I run a hand through my mullet,
and tug on the acid-washed jean
jacket that's my trademark, my look.

With a wink into a lonely mirror, I forego the
closet-clean out
−for now.

Living forever might create too much clutter,
too much junk, but I choose the creeping
collections of other people's stuff because who
knows what will be back in fashion once again,
and I am always in style.

Love You to Death

Oh Death, I miss you.
I want you.
It's been so long.

I ache to feel the last seconds
of heavy air expelling from my lungs
under your all-encompassing, cold
embrace.

When we last met, you
held me on the untouched grass, the
dew pressed into my face,
your hand over my mouth.
My last scream forever silenced.

Death, where have you gone?
You left me here all alone.
It's been an age. I still miss you.

Consumption

To consume is the best part
of American culture. Buy more
to save more, some implore.

Luckily for me, I don't have to spend
any cash for the things I need
to feed and clothe myself.

I take from the willing would-
be-victim and the unsuspecting passerby.
It matters not.

I drink my fill, check the wallets and
the pocketbooks and move on
to the next.

It's true; I consume more than most
and pay a hefty price,
if a soul costs anything.

To My Maker

Birthing a new vampire
takes time, effort, care.
I became a partner to you, a friend,
a lover, too.

It's not unusual for us
to hunt together, to find the same
things amusing. We are made from
one another, forever entwined.

In the dark, I proudly walk by your side—
by day, I worry when we hide and slink away.
It's always the same, though. I know we won't
grow old, but we'll be together, always.

A Vampire in Versace

Street style flutters here and there from the non-stop
blowing of hot air from the catwalks
of New York and Milan.

No mortal ever wears the over-the-top
art pieces meant to launch new collections
or makeovers for old houses.

But Versace, for Vampires, finds
welcome (under)takers each year.

The safety pin dress still wows, but
Donatella's bondage ensemble is the one
we all want.

Fangs, Wings, and Whores

Walking down Bourbon Street
gives tourists a look at the best
and worst of New Orleans.

The sights, the sounds, the
smells all tempt or repulse
depending on the amount
of alcohol in the system.

Playing the part of a vampire
and being a vampire are
two different things, but
here, it seems not to matter.

If you wear the fake fangs,
you are welcome.

The angel wings fluttering above the crypts
attempt to wave the unworthy along.

Weight Watcher

In a former life my
meal prepping stole time
from other forms of self
abuse like Big Macs and Dairy
Queen drive thrus.

Planning each bite
came with a discounted price—
a lack of time to finish all that
life required.

I spent Saturdays shopping
and then chopping green peppers
into thin strips and peeling
tiny cucumbers.

After the washing up,
I was too tired to slit
my wrists, veins blue—
and pulsing.

So the cycle repeated,
week after week.

It's a shame,

really. The constant rotation
of food preparation
kept me from focusing on the danger
nearby. My expiration date

ironically appeared at the
dark side of the Safeway–
since I was a perfect meal
prepared for one with discerning taste.

Dear---,

I was scared and seventeen when you took me.
You were gentle and kind, more so than I deserved.
I never chose this life—neither did you, truth be told. I
am always going to be seventeen now, no matter the
years that pass. I watch the seasons swirl by
one after the next. It's been four springs since you died,
again. I wonder when I will stop looking for you.

--J

Yesferatu

A leading man as a movie
vampire demands attention.

The character, forever
remembered, encases the

star in the unnatural
celluloid glow.

When the costumes portray the
way the plot might go,

the marketing takes over;
the audience prepares.

Is it a period drama with
lace collars and ruffles?

Or is it gritty, dirty, and
filled with unending pleather?

If the vampires don't sparkle,
I'm there.

Cut

I held the wound tight.
It bled in angry spurts
leaking through my fingers.

I put the bandage in my hand;
the flesh opened under the white gauze
turning into pink lumps of wasted

effort. I applied failing pressure.

You took my hand away and squeezed
it tight, for a second.

Then, I let go.

A Solar Eclipse

For the chance to glimpse the
orb denied to me, I'll risk the fates.

And I'm hungry.

The countdown begins, 10, 9, 8, 7
6, 5, 4, 3, 2, 1.

The whoops and cheers erupt.

I find the quiet ones in lawn chairs.
No one hears them whimper.

In under four minutes, I have
my fill. I take in the ring of fire, what's left of the sun,
before slithering back underground.

My Name

My name is a mystery to me.

It's been too long since I've heard it as an address.

I forget the sound of it on a lover's tongue. The memory
of the letters hanging on the sides of their lips
or hitting the top row of teeth when it's spoken in a
whisper
still means something to me.

A name is the first gift a parent bestows.
It's a burden, with baggage and strings,
tied to others. Cutting connections
and losing all haunts me in this existence.

Some call me a god as they lean into the embrace
of death, my hand pushing the empty-eyed face away.

Others call me a devil when they first see the glint
in my eyes and the flash of my fangs.

While a god or devil might be my true nature
—my calling—
a name seems too human,

too unsettling.

For now, remembering my name gives
me hope. Maybe my humanity rests inside the name.

Maybe.

Sharks

Great White Sharks shine with beauty, grace,
and teeth.

I find them fascinating, honorable,
high praise from one predator to another.

They won't hurt you if you leave
them alone, some research says.

I know better.

As I write this,
one just bit someone in Australia.

"A Pleasure for Fiends"

For Bram

It seems like pleasure for fiends—
the watching, the living, the waiting
for the next few scenes of tragedy
on a movie screen.

The action exists for the audience's overall rating.
The gloomy plot misleads,
but it just seems like cheap pleasure for fiends.

The villains, monotonous and continually alive,
entertain millions. While audiences hate
the monster and wait for the hero to proceed
with the overall scheme,

it's just more pleasure for fiends.

The damsels faint, the walls fold in, the Gothic breeds
an undying disease,
translating love into hate for all the villagers watching.

www.ingramcontent.com/pod-product-compliance
Lightning Source LLC
Chambersburg PA
CBHW051001030426
42339CB00007B/424